HARD INSTRUMENTAL (SAD/EDGY)

Refined*

Shivers up my spine,
I can't make up my mind,
Oh, I'm asking "Why?"
Looking upward to the sky...
Infect me with your iris.
You infect me with your iris.
Refined like diamonds I found out in the desert.
You haunt me, but I let you inside all the time.
Tonight, it's you and I.
With shivers up my spine.
I've got shivers up my spine.
Shivers up my spine.
I've got shivers up my spine.
I don't want to hide.
I can't make up my mind.
Looking up, I'm asking "Why?"
Upward to the sky.
I don't want to lie.
I want to see you try until the end of time.

Until the end of time.
I try to sleep at night. I can't shut my eyes.
I've been praying patiently, when I just want to cry.
I don't want to die, but God, I love your light.
Until the end of time.
With shivers up my spine.
I've got shivers up my spine.
All I see if you and I.

I Love You (E) *
Tell me what you said.
You think that you're through.
Even full of terror, I think I could love you.
I fly away, oh, I'm due.
I'd kind of like to get this through my head.
You think we're through.
You think I'm a servant, I tell you that it's true.
I fly away, but I want to find you.
I'd kind of like to.
I love you.
I love you.

I've been up all night, baby.
Is our forever through?
Is this the silver lining?
Is this the truth?
Tell me what you said, baby.
Could we be together, too?
Is this the end?
I thought we'd be "forever", too.
I love you.
I love you.
Creature.
Creature, tell me what you find.
Don't be too unkind.
Tell me all your stories, each and every
kind.
Silently at night. (Silently at night)
We can say it all, we can lose our minds.
Tell me what you are, tell me what you
like.
You've been on the line, you've been out
of line.
Let me bleed my heart, let me bleed my
spine.
Creature, tell me what you find.
Don't be too unkind.

Tell me all your stories, each and every kind.
Silently at night. (Silently at night)
There's a perk that we all can find.
Oh, my little light, don't be too unkind.
You can pour the sugar, salt on all the lime.
For all your life, for all your life.
So creature, tell me what you find.
Don't you be too scared, don't you run and hide.
I'll give you all my heart, I'll sacrifice my time.
Silently at night. (Silently at night.)
Paralyzed.
Below the sun.
Below the rain.
Below my eye horizon.
My glassy gaze, your infection fragrance.
I don't need to taste the fame...
So, it's another show.
I know, I don't want to go.
We all bear secrets, we all bear pain.
Look me in the eyes, I feel the same.
I've been paralyzed.

Pieces of my mind, they've been
hypnotized.
Hypnotized and paralyzed!
 Paralyzed.
I've been paralyzed.
By victimizing eyes, I've been
hypnotized.
Hypnotized and paralyzed.
Paralyzed.
Can you see my past?
My mistakes?
How I'm a fire upon horizons.
My pressing daze, your infectious face.
I want to make it through the day.
Woah, we're moving on and up.
Don't leave me in the rut.
Please share your secrets, and share your
pain.
I want to feel it all again!
I've been paralyzed.
Pieces of my mind, they've been
hypnotized.
Hypnotized and paralyzed!
 Paralyzed.
I've been paralyzed.

By victimizing eyes, I've been hypnotized.
Hypnotized and paralyzed.
Paralyzed.
Below the surface, below the face, and below my eye's horizon .
My classic daze, and your infectious fragrance.
I don't need to play your games.
Look me in the eyes, while we've got today!
I Fucking Adore You.
Tell me all you've ever known and what you've shown and how you grow.
Turn off all the episodes and see the world I want to know.
Tell me all you've ever known, it's sweetness seeping in my bones and I can't picture simple eyes, I know you're out there, keep on trying.
From breath breaks to shorelines.
To melodies and base lines.
Convenience stores and hate crimes.
Prom post-scripts to brain-wise.
I don't want to bore you.
I fucking adore you.

They say I'm dying.
I tell them all I'm fine.
I don't want to bore you
I fucking adore you.
They say I'm lying
When I tell them all I'm trying
I'll tell you all it's what you know and
what you've shown and how you grow.
Turn off all the episodes and see the
world I want to know.
Tell me all you've ever known.
It's sweetness seeping in my bones.
I can't picture simple minds.
I know you're out there, keep on trying.
From all of the skylines to all of the
streetlights.
 I'll keep trying.
I'll sing with the sky.
I don't want to bore you.
I fucking adore you.
They say I'm dying.
I tell them all I'm fine.
I don't want to bore you.
I fucking adore you.
They say I'm dying.
I tell them all I'm fine.

Battle.
Once I was told to behold the night and all of the ones seem mad at me.
I'm battle.
Soldier, stomp your feet into the earth.
Don't be scared, I'm here, my dear.
I've been told to incite, and assemble all of the ones seem passionate.
I'm battle.
Soldier, stop, take a breath, and take a hold.
Don't be scared. I'm here, My Dearest.
I won't let you go.
No, I won't let you go, now.
I might let you know.
I'm battle.
I'll March On.
I'll march on. (And on, and on.)
Oh, my love. (Above, above.)
See my home. (A home, a home.)
Long ago. (Ago, ago.)
Oh, I know. (I know, I know.)
All these souls. (From soul to soul.)
Here I go! (I go, I go!)
Not alone! (Alone, alone.)
I'll march on. (And on, and on.)

Oh, my love. (Above, above.)
See my home. (A home, a home.)
Long ago. (Ago, ago.)
Oh, I know. (I know, I know.)
All these souls. (From soul to soul.)
Here I go! (I go, I go!)
Hear my song! (A song, a song)
I Wish That I Knew You
I feel weak and I'm burning my
weekends.
My friends, I can't see them.
Can't be them...
Don't need them...
So funny...
No money...
You're sweet, like honey, I wish we could
dance like we used to.
I wish that I knew you.
Valentine's Day
Baby, I've been wondering, I'm waiting
for that call.
You've been on my mind, in the summer
and the fall.
Last winter and spring, we were dancing
to stranger songs.

Are you ready now? We have got to go.
Take me to a land I can call my forever
home.
Grass so green where people never
roam...
We were chasing dreams, racing cars,
and love took us to the stars.
You, the moon. I'll be Mars.
It was Valentine's Day.
On Valentine's Day...
We can go south, or we can take a train.
We can go to Hood, we've got gloves,
hats, and friends.
We can be anything.
We can do anything.
We can think anything.
We can see everything.
Oh my dreamer, I've been cold.
Steal my heart and steal my soul.
Beautiful dreamer, I've been cold.
Steal my heart and steal my soul.
Oh my dreamer, meet my all.
See my heart and see my soul.
Beautiful dreamer, be my friend.
Hear my mark, and, here, my hand.
Would It Kill To Want Me?

Would it kill to want me?
I'm not just your sorry sidepiece.
Would it kill to talk?
You got this story wrong between all
your friends and all your talking.
I don't have time for you.
Don't start walking.
We were better when we were together.
A letter from you would be better than
fake ass smiles.
You wont lie to me, hold my hand, you
can cry to me.
Would it kill to want me? I'm not just
some sorry sidepiece.
Would it kill to talk? This broken road is
so damn long.
You know you haunt me.
Smoke away my hopeless fantasy.
Would it kill to talk?
Would it kill to talk to me?
Tell Me How You Feel.
Tell me what you said...
Is my forever through?
I don't want to lose you.
I don't want to fly away again.
Would you give me your pain?

Give me your secrets?
I will hold them, I will keep them.
What's this feeling, now, is it intimate?
Can you wait for me, can you wait a bit?
And tell me how you feel when no one is
around.
Tell me how you're feeling ten feet off
the ground.
You're so beautiful.
I'd kind of like to tell you.
I'd kind of like forever too.
I'd kind of like to tell you we could fly
forever, too.
I'll be your voice when you can't find
your own.
Through the worst of times, and the rest.
We'll be unstoppable, we won't ever fall,
my friend.
Would you give me your pain?
Give me your secrets?
I will hold them, I will keep them.
What's this feeling, now, is it intimate?
Can you wait for me, can you wait a bit?
And tell me how you feel when no one is
around.

Tell me how you're feeling ten feet off
the ground.
You're so beautiful.
Tell me how you feel when no one is
around.
Tell me how you want to sink into the
sound.
You're so beautiful.
This is what I know, baby
I think that it's overdue.
I think I love you
I won't fly away again.
Borderline Broken
I gave it all, for you.
I broke my own heart in two.
Do you see, when I sleep, my life is in
color.
These stars inside me burn.
I did it all, for you.
I'll give it all, for you.
Do you still want me?
Do you still love me?
Don't hurt me...
Don't hurt me anymore.
Oh, you tear me to pieces.
It's so rare to see glimpses of you.

Someone send me off to a place I can find myself.
My mental health is borderline broken.
I'm borderline broken, and so are you.
I'm borderline broken.
I'm borderline broken, thanks, to you.
Do you still want me?
Do you still love me?
Don't lie to me...
Don't lie to me anymore.
I gave it all for you.
I broke my own heart in two.
Do you still love me?
Don't hurt me anymore.
Daddy.
Daddy doesn't drink, she ain't picking up the phone.
It's sad to see the things I don't really want to know.
He doesn't like to talk, she doesn't really want to go and you've been thinking hard, I've been thinking not at all.
Daddy doesn't sing. Daddy doesn't give a fuck.
He was working late. She was dancing at a bar.

He doesn't really know just how to think before he talks.
So he had to take a walk.
Why'd I need you to ever care at all.
Every night you don't ever want to talk.
So damn high, I don't ever want to fall, no.
You don't really want to know.
You don't care at all.
Daddy took a hit. Daddy loaded up a bowl.
Daddy broke a needle in his motherfucking throat
She doesn't like to see just what he's doing all alone.
You don't really want to know.
He doesn't want to think. She don't want no fucking smoke.
Daddy praying hard, daddy's losing all his hope.
Daddy sleeping outside, he's so fucking cold.
He's so fucking cold.
Why'd I need you to ever care at all.
I might need to run or fucking crawl.
Ocean waves crash upon the shore.

And you don't really want to know.
He's wasting his life, he doesn't really want to go.
Looking for a brother or a sister or a home.
Daddys thinking hard, now he's picking up the phone.
But you don't really want to know.
You don't really want to know.

Morning Star

Morning light comes, and I'm waiting for you.
Is this the hour that I find you alone?
Was this our secret or was it all told?
Will we keep going as the wheels roll along?
Sticks and stones won't break my heart...
Will you break my heart?
I'll be damned if I do, and damned if I don't.
Put down the guns and put down the rum.
I'll only know if I give up this line drawn in the sand in between us.
Laying alone, still praying for you.
Do I see you?

Do I need you?
 Have I been lost in my mind and the
phone?
Am I alone, no...
Sticks and stones won't break my heart.
Would you break my heart?
Brittle as bone, with the weight of the
world.
I'll let it unfurl.
I'll be damned if I do, and damned if I
don't.
Put down the guns and put down the
rum.
I'll only know if I give up this line drawn
in the sand in between us.
What's in between us?
Still, the morning light comes.
Still, a raindrop could shake us.
Still, steady, both our hearts beating.
I hear you within.
I'll be damned if I do, and damned if I
don't.
Put down the guns and put down the
rum.
I'll only know if I give up this line drawn
in the sand in between us.

Flow

Tell me what you want.
Tell me what you need.
I could be it all, or I could let you
breathe.
I've seen this other side, now I want to
see you.
I think I need you.
I believe, so go—-
You want to go—
Your dreams are yours.
I feel your words.
Baby, flow—
Just flow—
Refine your soul.
Define it all.
Tell me what you said, baby.
Is our forever through?
You think I'm a servant?
I think I could love you.

Lonely As Can Be

Don't stop popping.
Now don't stop locking.
Keep your feet off the dance floor, and
I'll keep rocking.
Fly like a bird, I'm as lonely as a bee.

My mother thinks that I'm as happy as
can be.

Know, How

People here, people poor.
People here I know.
Know, how?
People think, and they throw.
People here, I know.
Not alone.
People tall, people old.
People hear my woe.
Woah, now.
People come, people go.
People seed and they sew.
So now.
People here, they grow.
People here, I know.
Know, how?

Wrangler

Hold my hand through the night.
We can soar.
We can fly.
With you I can fall asleep.
Here's my life.
Here's my dream.
Is this impossible?

I want to do the impossible.
Do you love me?
Do you need me?
Do you care?
Don't you see?
We can be high.
We can be free!
Let's go ride!
Is this impossible?
I want to do the impossible.
ROCK (POETIC/LOVE)

Ocean Man*
Come to life.
I need you to come to life.
Harmonize.
You feel the rhythm just harmonize.
I get pulled into your lull and trance.
Intricate dances, and sideways glances.
On the sand, I'm just one man..
Take my hand, take my hand.
Understand, please, understand.
Understand, understand.
Understand, please, understand.
Understand, understand.
You've heard a lot.
You're still until the beat drops.

I can not get down unless you're down to talk.
So come to life.
Bring your sweetness into my life.
Harmonize, to the rhythm, just harmonize.
From "I'll have this dance." to "Here I stand."
We still can, baby, we still can.
On the sand, please, take this hand.
Take this hand, take this hand.
Understand, please, understand.
Understand, understand.
Understand, please, understand.
Understand, understand.
Can you capture me?
Lead me, baby, all for me?
Like gravity, you pull me in like gravity.
From the punk rock bands to the one night stands.
Read my hands, read my hands.
I'll be there, I'll be your biggest fan.
Take my hand, take my hand.
Understand.
Understand, please, understand.
100,000 miles

Are you ok? You up now? You want to see the world and be a part of the ones that you've always seen in spotlights. A tremble, a tremolo, a race car drifting through the dust now, the dust now, the dust now, I'm dust.
You ok? You ok? Should I stay or go right now?
A bass line, a hate crime, a drifter nomad-land.
You ok? You ok?
Should I try to get a little bit competitive, repetitive, inventive, in lust.
I can see right who you are, you're not gonna die. I swear on my makeshift game of a little bit of time, I'll walk one hundred thousand miles. To let you. To get you. To bet on a match I'll set you.
You ok? You ok? You ok? I don't think we've been too ok...
Too ok...Too ok...Too ok...
You up now? You up now? You want to be a part of all the fuss now? The break downs? The queen-like crowns and strife?

A rumble, a fumble, a point I'll take into
the newfound night crowd, full of night
gowns, to the light now, I see white.
The comedown, the letdown, the bet
now, bet now. A bed now, a bed now. I
want to get inside your head, now,
I can see right who you are, you're not
gonna die I swear on my makeshift game
my makeshift lines, I'll walk one
hundred thousand miles.
One hundred thousand miles.
From fairy tales and ferry men to birds
in the sky.
From ruins and Roman cavalry, to words
of every type.
From Robin Hood to men in uniforms,
black and white.
From books of prayer and poses to roses
for Valentines.
From road signs to stop signs, we benefit
from time.
From cocktails to mocktails made dirty
with the lime.
The twisted and the wicked fight with
heroes and the gods.

These words, they can shape your every move and every thought.
Future Youth of mine, I want to see you shine.
You can tell your stories to the ones you find alike.
For creed and creeping vines.
For fights and favorite wine.
You become a memory like what was sung at night.
Future Youth of mine, I want to see you smile.
You can tell the ones who hope to stay a while.
For creed and creeping vine.
For fate and future lines.
You become a memory like planets in the sky.

Coming Apart*
You can scream and call like sirens and thunder.
You can't make sense of it all, but you can uncover.
Skin and bone, cold like old blue jeans.
Can you show me how to lose control?

While you're still standing, still stuck in
a trance.
Eyes demanding.
Take my hand, through all of the dark.
All, I am here for you.
While I'm still standing, and still stuck
in a trance, I'll be here for you.
The sunlight is shining, and I'm stuck in
a trance.
Your eyes, they're shining.
So take my hand, through all of the dark.
I am here for you while you're coming
apart.
Woah.
Oh.

Connected Souls.
I pray to you and I.
I'm not the one.
I feel the world, how it runs so cold.
To the skies above, and the ground
below, my bodies are all I might ever
know.
But I pray to you and I.
I'm not the only one.
I feel your love, how it ebbs and flows.

To the skies above, and the ground
below, my bodies all connected souls.
C'est La Vie!
You can get addicted to an anthem.
You can get addicted to a way.
You can fall in love with a phantom.
You can fall in love with the pay.
You can get addicted to the madness
I was addicted to whatever she would say
So starve off all of the sadness.
Start to see the light of day. Light your
day and–
C'est la vie! Say you love me, we could
dance up in the dark!
All for me? All for nothing...All for being
all a part...
Bring me up! Bring me time! Tired of
this animosity I see!
 I might go somewhere you will never
find...
Drink up! Carbon wine!
Spirits might just shake you! So new! So
divine!
So surrender to the harmony, la vie!
C'est la vie!
You can get addicted to an enemy.

You can get addicted to the bank.
You can get addicted to the bitter cold
and you can get addicted to the sweet hot
day.
You can get addicted to an anthem.
I was addicted to whatever she would
say.
I'll build up one, just to smile.
I'll build you up just to say–
C'est la vie! Say you love me!
We could dance up in The dark!
All for me? All for nothing... All for being
all a part.
Bring me up! Bring me time! Tired of
this animosity I see!
I might go somewhere you will never
find!
Drink up! Carbon wine! Drink the spirits
that might shake us!
So new! Sublime! Surrender to the
harmony, la vie!
C'est la vie!

Be My Love
You don't need to know that you're
beautiful, we're surrounded by the words
that make us feel so small.

They'll beat you down, reform you to submission.
I'm not looking for an angel, just somebody to listen.
You don't have to love all of the people.
You can change your mind.
You can change your life.
My clock is ticking.
My heart is gold.
My body is numb.
I'm growing old.
I got a beat up guitar and worn out strings, and a million other pointless things.
My mother, I never get to see, and daddy's still rocking his light blue jeans.
My clock is ticking. My heart is worn.
I swear I felt an angel. I hear her mourning.
She got a beat up guitar and worn out strings and a million other pointless things.
But, here I stand, I'm still chasing dreams.
For You.
Don't you know I would die, for you?

Don't you know I'll be there for you?
Don't you know I would stay by your
side?
Don't you know wherever I am, wherever
I go, whenever the clock stands still I
know, Forever, I'll cry for you.
Forever I'll try for you.
Wherever you fall, wherever I know,
whenever our hearts through sunlight
show, Forever, I'll cry for you.
Forever, I'll try for you.
For you... For you...
Don't you know, I'd never lie to you.
Don't you know, I would fly to you.
Don't you know, I'm here by your side?
Wherever you are, wherever you go,
whenever you're lost, whenever you're
cold, Forever, I'll cry for you.
Forever, I'll try for you.
Wherever you fall, wherever I know,
whenever our heartbeats sync or stop,
Forever, I'll cry for you.
Forever I'll try for you.
For you... For you..
For you.... For you...
Forever.

The lonely rebel with a big heart.
Tall tale, you can go where you want to.
 I never wanted all the glam or the race
cars.
I never meant to hurt you.
Yesterday was a late start.
Tell me what I could have done to make
a difference in a world full of deep scars.
Oh, deep scars.
You've got deep scars.
Deep scars... I see deep scars.
Is it someone you know?
Or is it someone you've told?
Forever I'll ask.
Forever I'll ask you.
Is it something you hold?
Maybe diamond or gold?
Forever I'll ask you.
Forever I'll ask you.
Oh... I want to go far.
I want to fly, I want to take you all with
me.
You don't have to compare yourself.
You don't have to be perfect.
You don't have to be stuck in the past.
I'm only a human.

I can be what I want to.
Woah, I see deep scars...
Deep scars.
You've got deep scars..
I'm still a rebel with a big heart
We all fight, we can go where we want to.
Close your eyes, and know you played a big part.
When you're looking for a new start, when your looking for a friend, here, I got you.
When you're flying with the race cars.
You don't need another deep scar.
I see deep scars.
Woah, deep scars.

When I'm Not Around
Beautiful blood, they say you've got to help yourself.
People that I knew, how they echo through the clouds.
Through the tears, I won't let them get me down.
I think that I'm stronger now.
I feel it in my heart, I feel it in your vows.

Fill me up with promises, please don't
rip them out.
I don't want to run, I've been running
through the town.
Oh, I'll tell you when I'm not around.
Either way I love it, now, bottles up and
button downs.
Here's a memory of people that I follow
now.
Light me through the dark, show your
scars to the town.
I think that I'm stronger now, I'll tell
you when I'm not around.

All I Ever Wanted

I know I'm not the only one on your
mind.
Some things are hard to say.
Some things are hard to face.
I can't remember what you said that
night.
Today's another day.
Go ahead, go crazy.
I've got to run now.
I can't keep crawling.
In my mind, I still hear you calling.
I'm still rolling.

I can't keep falling.
In my mind, now, you're all I ever
wanted.
I know I'm not that perfect all the time.
Is it Heaven I walk, or Hell, I can't
decide.
From thunder clouds to open sunny
skies.
From the best of the worst, and the
worst of the best of life.

I know I'm going crazy all night.
But, today's another day.
Lift up your chin and say it.
I've got to run now.
I can't keep crawling.
In my mind, I still hear you calling.
I'm still rolling.
I can't keep falling.
In my mind, now, you're all I ever
wanted.

Old Fighter

Simmer down and keep it low. Burning
pure and seeing gold. The people here,
they could know. Don't forget or let it go.

Just keep me close with beaten clothes and raindrops on the rooftops.
Keep my woes and warm my soul and settle down old fighters.
From mountaintops to riverbeds and getting lost inside our heads. We are strong and we are old. We are brass and we are bone, so keep me close with beaten clothes and raindrops on the rooftops.
Keep my woes and warm my soul and settle down old fighters.
Breaking stride and breaking bone. Calling skies before the phone. Asking why, but I don't know, I'm keeping time and seeing all that keeps me close with beaten clothes and raindrops on the rooftops.
Keep my woes and warm my soul and settle down old fighters.
Take me higher.
Mirror of Mine.
Mirror of mine, both shattered and bright, show the pieces, show me the signs.
Beautiful Mind.

Don't you be down, lift up your eyes.
Lift up your voice, say to the sky "You'll
be alright."
I won't be scared, I won't be blind.
It might take courage and it might take
time.
You'll feel alive.
Mirror of mine, both shattered and
bright, show me the secrets and show
me the signs.
Beautiful Mind.
Don't you be down, lift up your eyes, lift
up your spirit and sing with the sky.
You'll be alright.
Don't be too scared, don't tread too
lightly.
Show us your courage and show us all
why.
You'll feel alive.

Lakeside

I hope you know I love you, and I hope
you know just why we treasure all of the
moments.
I think of you and smile.
I think of you, so fine.
Underneath umbrellas by the lakeside.

You can pick your cherry by the lakeside.
I'd love to play this loud just like you'd
love to sing so high.
Treasure all the people that you see
through your life.
I hope you know I hold you so damn
close all the time.
Underneath umbrellas by the lakeside.
You can pick your cherry by the lakeside.
I hope you know I love these open roads
and city skylines.
I hope you know I love all of your curves,
and all of your lines.
Underneath umbrellas by the lakeside.
You can pick your cherry by the lakeside.
(Underneath umbrellas by the lakeside.)
(You can pick your cherry by the
lakeside.)

Hold Me Tight (F)
Turn off the lights.
I'll take the wheel and I'll hold it all
night.
Wherever you go, I'm here for the ride.
Just let me know, just hold me tight.
Softly, I whisper.
 Come closer, closer.

Just feel my heart, now, it will not lie.
Wherever you go, I'm here for the ride.
Just let me know, just hold me tight.
These streets get me high.
Just hold my hand and I'll take you to
paradise.
Wherever you go...
I'm here for the ride.
Just let me know...
Oh, please, hold me tight.

Ms. IV

I'm not a saint. (No, I'm not a saint.)
Caught in the rain. (We were caught in
the rain.)
Numb me away. (You're like novocaine.)
Ms. Intra-vein, oh, Ms Intra-vein.
I'm not a saint, I'm not a teacher.
I miss the days up on the bleachers.
I miss the days... (I miss the days...)
Last summer break, I caught a fever.
Out in the rain, just to see her.
Staying up late. (You know I'm up late.)
I don't want to hide, I won't run away.
It's hard to find a less paved way.
Light up the pain, you know it's insane.
I'm not a saint. (I'm not a saint.)

I miss the day. (I miss the day)
Staying up late. (You know I'm up late)
Ms. Intra-vein. (Oh, Ms. Intra-vein.)
Last break. (Last summer break.)
Out in the rain. (We were out in the rain.)
Staying up late. (You know I'm up late)
Ms. Intra-vein. (Oh, Ms. Intra-vein.)

Hilltops

I know you told me once before that we would be alright rich or poor.
Can I sing you a simple song?
A simple song, dear, a simple song.
I just want to shout it from the hilltops.
Run away with all I've ever known.
I don't need to stay to make a fortune of your heart is all I carry in my soul.
I know you gently, I know you so.
I knew you way back then, how we grow.
Can I sing you a simple song?
A simple song, now, a simple song.
I just want to shout it from the hilltops.
Run away with all I've ever known.
I don't need to stay to make a fortune of your heart is all I carry in my soul.
For all I am now, for all I was.

For all I know below and above.
I want to sing you a simple song.
A simple song, a simple song.
I just want to shout it from the hilltops.
Run away with all I've ever known.
I don't need to stay to make a fortune of
your heart is all I carry in my soul.
I want to run, now, I want to go.
I want to keep it all, keep it close.
I want to sing you a simple song.
A simple song, dear. A simple song.
I just want to shout it from the hilltops.
Run away with all I've ever known.
I don't need to stay to make a fortune of
your heart is all I carry in my soul.
No Expectations.
Searching earth with no expectations.
Hurting myself, with no expectations.
I've been running through my mind, it's
all been changing.
It's all been changing.
I need some time.
I need a pen.
I won't give up, I promise, my friend.
Inside my mind everything's changing.
I'll rearrange it.

Like many before, infinicy, I adore you.
So true the things that you do.
Like many before, darkness, I adore you.
So blue, the things you do.
Toast to the lost with nowhere to go.
Toast to songs on repeat, everywhere I go.
I've been running through my head.
I've been running, in my head.
I've been running through my mind, it's all been changing.
I'll rearrange it.
Like many before, infinicy, I adore you.
So true the things that you do.
Like many before, darkness I adore you.
So blue, the things that you do.
I've been searching this earth
God, will I make it?
Help me see my true self, now.
I've been running through my mind with no expectations.
No expectations.
To: All That I See
I won't forget you.
Deep within time you bury your lines, I see you above.

In my mirror I see your smile still at my
side.
This reflection has said:
To all that I see, and all that I meet.
Fall and I'll catch you, I'm here till the
end.
Here for the highs and here for the pains.
Here for the moments we'll never forget.
To all that I see, keep going and hoping.
Grow like the earth, till the end.
We're here for the highs and here for the
pains.
I'll never forget.
Strong with spirit.
 Don't be afraid.
I'll always give time to a friend on the
line and to the heavens creating me.
In this life I find this road I walk alone.
I just want to walk it again.

Tokyo

I'll buy us electric motors and foreign
houses.
I'd dream up a life we like.
I get caught in all the motion, darling.
It seems we've got a story to tell the sky.

I'm married to the earth, married to the ocean, married to the ones I love, and I try to be more than just a moment.
I'll fly us to Tokyo and all the shorelines.
I'll dream up a life we like.
Momma, you can understand me, ang tu sabes.
When I got lost, you found me, oh how I...
Oh, I'd buy us a hundred million dollar houses.
I'd dream up a life we like.
I'll never let the love die.
I'm married to the earth.
I'm married to the ocean.
I'll never forget the ones I love, and I'll never let go of the ones that make the moments.
You make the moments.
Fly us to Tokyo and all the shorelines.
Dream up a life you like
Tell me you can understand me, when I cry
When I got lost, you found me, oh how I...
ALTERNATIVE (HAPPY/UPBEAT)

My Heart

We are like water and fire. We are like
moss and stone
We are the hope and future. We won't be
long.
Maybe we can feel, again.
Maybe it's a deal, again.
I think we'll learn to be again.
I think we'll learn to see again.
In your car, look out and see the stars.
They're all ours, I'll let them be a part.
I'm never far. You've had a beautiful
start.
To your heart.
To your heart.
Where you've been.
Roll down and feel the wind.
 I want to take you to places you've never
been.
I'm never far.
You've been a beautiful part.
To your heart.
To your heart.
We are like changing seasons. We are the
dust and bone.

We can be here and now, until we're
called back to home.
I'm learning how to fly again.
 I just want to try again.
I think we'll learn to be again.
I think we'll learn to feel again.
Autumn in August
Autumn in August, twirling and frayed.
Leaf piles up, we had a luck streak.
Hymnals and prayers, confessions and
fragrance.
 You walk a road that I've been on.
Maybe it's a part of the secrets we are
not the perfect people the world thinks
we are.
Even in the dark, your a song to my heart
beat, the wind to my sails and I say.
Please stay.
Please say everything you think of me.
Do you think of me?
From coast-line, to coast-line, nothing
in our way.
We started fires for fun, in my day.
I hear you like to dance, we can dance all
night long.
You walk a road that I've been.

Maybe together were worn down and weathered but still, you might pull me along
It's been a long time, I've got pennies and dimes, but still, I feel you belong.
It's Autumn in August, with willow and hay.
Lattes and long late night drives on the highway.
We locked our eyes, as we parted, that day.

I Do Not

One thing I know.
I don't love you.
I don't hate you.
I won't fuck you.
I don't work no 9–5, I can't stand or breathe right.
Share your blessings. Dare yourself, dear.
One thing I know.
I don't love you.
I don't hate you.
I won't fuck you.
One thing I know.
I might hug you.
I don't hate you.

I won't fuck you.
Be My Love (Em, G)
Baby, are you mean, on the low?
I could bring green (on the low).
Fit so clean I'm in love
Fit so clean I'm in love
Be my drug.
Baby, please take my hand.
I just want to see you again.
I'll see you again.
I just want to be your man.
Be your man.
Be my friend.
It's raining, I'm humming, I'm at the corner of 4th and Burnside.
I'm asking someone to run up into the tavern, buy me a drink again.
It's a pattern. You were the baddest.
You were the baddest.
I am crazy, I'm bumming, I lack all of the love and all of the chatter.
I've been away, I've been gone, but I'm back. Up my defense cause you're my attack.
You were the baddest.
You were the baddest.

On my arm I got cool tat. Can you just
love me the way that I am?
I've been around, I'm doing the math.
Seeing the path, feeling the wrath.
Tell me it matters. Tell me I matter.
Baby, are you mean, on the low?
I could bring green (on the low).
Fit so clean I'm in love
Fit so clean I'm in love.
Be my love.
Baby, are you mean on the low?
I can see it all on the floor.
Fit so clean I'm in love.
Fit so clean I'm in love.
Be my love.

Peace of Mind

Take time to feel alive. I forget most of
the lines.
I'll sell a quarter for a dime. I'll never
settle, never rest.
In the rhythm feelin' high. I've got to
know, I've got to try.
Make dreams come to life. Give them all
your very best.
I want to help you find that peace of
mind I never had.

Can't we try to empathize? Not pour from bottles by the bed.
You might find that peace of mind I never had.
Let's all try to empathize. Not drown in bottles by the bed.
From your smile to your disguise to those whispers in the night.
They said this life could be a prize, every morning when you rise.
So go ahead and tell me why you think you'll make it all alright.
From these folk songs and campfire talks, I'll share my life upon these open city skies.
Be Everything You Want To Be.
Feeling so free, you can stay for the weekend.
We go back and forth until the dew drops do drop.
Shining like diamonds in the rough.
Miles we've gone, we're all grown up.
We want to see what we all could be.
We don't have to worry, gather round and get up.

Don't weep in the nosebleed seats, your
haze, the daze, will do.
I am all I can be. I'll try to reach
I might fall through the seams, but I'll
never let go.
Spirit so free you can trust it with me.
We swing along this long broken road.
What a feat, oh, what a scene.
Let's move our feet, be crazy.
I hope we all meet, and I hope we all see
that we don't have to worry, gather
round and get up/
From sea-shore to sea, I'll keep my eyes
locked in on everything I want to be.
Be everything you want to be.

When You Come Around

Wake and wait.
Be calm and patient.
Don't toss and turn.
Just shape yourself.
You break, you hurt and ache.
You can show us all how you can pause
and play.
You have all day.
You can keep the fog at bay.

When you know your rightful way, take
one look and hold it closely.
When you are around, I want to help you
find yourself when you're around.
When you come around, I want to take
you to the world that I have seen, I
dream, believe me when I
Wake and jump in, nod and shake.
Dance and prod you, chance, I'll take.
Feels like fate or a famous fable.
But the names all change, insane, now,
when you are around I want to help you
find yourself when you're around.
When you come around, I want to take
you to the world that I have seen, I
dream, believe me when
 I see you come around.
(Where've you been lately?)
When you come around.
(I'm thinking you can save me.)
When you are around.
(Tell me, are we concrete?)
When you come around.
(You could be my baby.)
Baby...
Raise Your Head & Eyes.

Raise your head and eyes every day.
(Raise your head and eyes...)
We might buy the sunshine every day.
(I told the sun 'Shine!'...)
I woke up this morning, and smiled with
the rising sun.
I smiled with the rising sun, and said,
"When you grow up, sun– Will you tell
the morning 'Please smile with your
rising sun?'"
Raise your head and eyes every day!
(Raise your head and eyes!)
We can go to paradise every day.
(We can go to paradise...)
Happiness is that little smile.
Taking your time, you've got a while.
Marry the love and simple lines.
Marry the tunes you carry through your
life.
Raise your head and eyes every day!
(Raise your head and eyes!)
We might buy the sun shine every day...
(I told the sun 'Shine!')
Raise your head and eyes every day!
(Raise your head and eyes!)
We can go to paradise every day!

(We can go to paradise!)
I'm On My Way
Way beyond a green horizon, the
starlight's on us.
We can fly.
Roaming roads that you can find.
The clouds keep rolling with the moon
up high.
I'm on my way, for the brightest days,
I'll keep a steady pace.
Way beyond my open eyes, we can find
our paradise.
Open roads and an open mind.
The starlights shy so the sun can rise.
I'm on my way, for the coldest nights,
and the brightest days.
Up ahead, we can roll the dice.
Take our chances, take our time.
One more time, now!
One more time!
Lift me up into the sky!
I'm on my way.
Downtown.
Downtown, the comedown and night is
behind us, and so are the teardrops that
follow you and me.

Rest in my arms and rest in between the willow and the palm tree.
Am I forgotten?
Am I alone?
Am I a Human from Paris or Seoul?
Hush now, the comedown and night is behind us and so are the teardrops that fall down your cheek.
Rest in my arms and rest in between the willow and the palm tree.
Ease now, at ease.
Am I alone now?
Am I at home?
Am I a Human?

Table Tops

Oh, I'm jumping britches, shootin' Z's!
I slide down from my apple tree!
Two more days till Sunday, though I really must not ring em'!
Twelve down, up on table tops, I'm singing round the apple bottom lady I just met and I don't even want to think.
I'm just a boy, not ten toes down yet!
I've been lashing on myself .
 I know it's better than alternatives!

So I see you swinging and I'll never let it go...
Okay, I'll let it go!
Forgive and forget this! Might just need some rest.
 It's never far from over, but my over isn't yet.
Forgive and forget me!
 I just tied another willow tree, my finger got no ring, and I don't want to see you swinging!
One more day I'm not afraid, I've got to say down by the bank I saw my mirror image and thought I got no singing.
Up and down I'm all around, there's one more girl with button downs, I think that I just met you and I've got a lot of love.
I'm just a boy, not ten toes down yet!
I've been lashing on myself.
 I know it's better than alternatives!
So I see you swinging and I'll never let it go...
Okay, I'll let it go!
Forgive and forget this!
 Might just need some rest.

It's never far from over but my oven isn't yet.
Forgive and forget me!
I just tied another willow tree, my finger got no ring, and I don't want to see you swinging!

Let's Dance Again
You light me light fire, girl.
You lose yourself, my muse.
You look so pretty, there.
You turn me on, it's true.
They all want to know, they all want to see our lips lock.
Your eyes lock in on the dance floor.
Let's dance again!
Swing our hips to the trance again!
Let's dream again!
Close our eyes and feel again!
Champagne coming all night lit by this blacklight back drop, babe.
The way you smile, I hope this time we can all go up in flames.

Do extraordinary things—

What I might gain may be different in your mind, but still, gained.

My Commandments.

As a being of matter, I must understand the processes which create us, and reproduce, but, be careful, as reproduction takes fuel, and the fuel we have is a limited resource shared among many, so I must fuel myself wisely, and ensure those around do the same.

As a governing force that understands will, and evil, seek peace in the world around you, and do not feed into or be fed by those who might lead you from faith in yourself, as some will fear what you love, and what you are.

As a being of motion and time, respect both wisely, and find yourself among those who do as well, as there is much land to pass underneath you, and much time to be spent in your mind, and in your hands, and in places you have yet to discover, until anti-matter takes you. As an eye that can see, and remember what you have seen, be mindful not to waste precious moments, but see the world and how it speaks, and how it guides, and how others might walk it alongside you, and discover what your eyes have beheld.

As a mind that never ceases, rest well, as you are only as strong as your healthiest days, and as vivid as your most vibrant dreams.

Remember your unity, with all in creation, and your place through all of time, and how it is as significant as your experience might allow, and as great as your story might tell.

Remember yourself in all that you see, as one day, they might see you, and your roles might reverse, and how you might never truly grasp what lies beyond, so what lies in front of you should be preached, for the sake of yourself, and all that embody it.

If You Love Me, I Need A Good-Bye.

I think that the almost globally recognized "peace" sign, for me, became an "I love you".
I threw it over my shoulder, I used it to hide my own face.
Sometimes, its use was excessive, sometimes it was forgotten.
I used it as an interchangeable model of goodbyes.
Somehow, it is easier to show it than it is to say, and that is completely OK, because you and I can be different.
Regardless,
If you love me, I need a good-bye.
Asking Myself, and Another.
Are you on your own?
Are you a roamer?
Do you march over stones, and bones, and broken society?
Will I stand for people, and laws against evil, for creatures I see?
I wish... I could— ask you.
What *is* possible?
What *is* important?
Are you guided by hope in droves?

To those that don't see, do you guide?
Provide?
Do you keep yourself within lines?
Do you give yourself time?
I might... More than one, now, I see.
When We All Understand.
Three eyes, or three trees?
Three trees or three people?
Three people or souls?
We've come so far.
Maybe the message got lost in
translation.
As I cross my legs and look up, the birds
swoon, and leaves sway, and tell me
"Look!"
I speak for them, too.
I'm upset. I'm neglected.
I'm a person!
Give me rights!
They're upset.
They're neglected.
They're people.
For all I know, it was lost in translation.
Why.

O' Future, what do you know from my
eyes?
O' Past, please, come with me, all of the
time.
Where is this Heaven I've heard of?
Where is this Utopia that everyone sees?
Your voice can soothe me with its touch.
I was fulfilled, then.
Back in the day, when we kissed under
porch lights and snuck out of windows.
Back in the day, where walks home took
too long.
We were young, impatient and reckless,
yet still, we loved, and were loved.
We were tired, yet driven.
Never lacking ambition, or judgment, or
laughter or snacks.
We would beg, if not to be seen, then
heard, or inspired.
We were all together.
Together light the colors that bind the
sky to the sea or the motions that bind
your soul to my eye.
Like the papers that bound all our
notebooks and songbooks.

These roles we fill, well said and well
put, like a second place pedestal, medal,
or ribbon.
Just hear what the heart desires, and
love, and go get it with all of the
strength you can muster.
Content is the day, and the day's still
alive, if you're with it.
We were with it back then...
And different...
One.
Feeling alone , when surrounded by life.
Feeling peace– For them all, just peace.
Comfort, a new kind of sin, in a world
where birds freeze and fall out of the sky.
Land we all walk, and give names to, and
put tax on, like it was not meant for any.
These things hurt me.
The body.
The mind.
The world.
The Universe, to those that seek it,
respect it, that walk alongside it, that
speak out to others that govern their

own, but the ones which you might call
your own.
I'm in line.
I can laugh.
I look back at the oceans and rivers, and
sing, and cry, and accept when I'm
wrong.
How I wish all our hands were one.
All our voices, just one.
Fly With Me, One Moment.
Fly this earth with me, for a moment.
Share your strut.
Cherish these knee high shrubs.
Give love, for these scared, furry friends.
For these creatures in realms and sphere
confines.
For what, when peeled away, is just
beyond the horizon.
The light becomes blinding, it flashes
across your vision.
How bright, just your mind—
I stop, and hear the thump from the
boom-box next door.
The non-partisan discussions.
The genius solutions.

The process and imperfections that are
found on the screens.

I look around, and see a hazy hillside,
with the smoke in the air.
But, some child plays gleefully with the
gift his parents could afford, this year,
like the discount cardstock and tissue
paper.
I Will.
I pray for a world gone silent.
I hear.
He sees the way I dig myself deep into a
valley of despair.
How I could scream and nobody would
run to me.
How people trudge on, as life never
rests, and we all moan quietly as our
pains are multiplied.
We don't need to take pills or products
that produce potent predispositions,
prescribed by "pacifists".
But, to the people that have never tried...
Still, I try.

And the key of D Minor haunts my eardrums, and I wonder when you began to listen.
Never again do I wish to feel the anguish of a heartbreak...
I will.
Never again will I try to make the same mistakes...
I will.
Never again will I get these chances to seize, yet, each day, I feel pulled in one way.
So, I will.
Will you go out and see all the people that could love you?
That wish you had a few minutes?
I have years.
Will you stop for a second, some time, and shout "Hey!"
Not too friendly, or aggressive.
Try passionately.
Will you obey the laws that were written?
The ones that you write?
Your will is strong, you know.
It is free.

It entangles and leads us like salmon to spawn, or like rain to the ground. Sometimes, that rain freezes, and sometimes, I look up.
If you will, too...
Questions: A New Life.
What is this?
I opened my eyes to the brightness, my body wrapped tight, and too warm.
Where am I?
I glanced to the side, and saw shapes, some dull colors and things.
Who are you?
As I looked the other way.
I love you.
I thought.
I love you.
I thought back.
What are you?
Who am I?
Where is this?
She left, and came back, and looked down, and smiled.
I know.
I was scared.

I'm here.
Then, less so.
One day...
She began.
I thought *Thank You* when she finished,
and cried, because I had never in my life
heard anything so lovely.
Beyond Growing Up.
Never did I see bouncy castles becoming
house parties, and laughter becoming
fights.
Never did I guess that the sun would
keep shining on forever, since that
moment had felt all too special, in
memory.
My memories could be playful, my
memories could be sweet.
Carmel apples and gummy shark or
sunsets at the park.
Sometimes they got crazy, with police, or
with chases, or bonfires.
The parties where best-dressed won the
looks.
Some nights were all lessons, about
respect, about parenting, or young love.

I feel more lucky now than I did back
then.
And, now, I should feel lucky.
The people that raised me, that gifted
and granted me these moments, while,
back then, may not have been present,
are here now.
So I hope they will listen, and let our
questions guide the answers to what lies
beyond our own minds.
Somewhere.
Reception, somewhere...
For the great horned owls
And the ground mice we eat.
And the things they have yet to discover,
Seeing your words fly by memories I
have had—
You understand me.
I might tip my hat, now and again, or
smile.
New conclusions and judgment, for us all.
Some grip racquets, others, guns.

And in the suburbs that tuned in to the
chaos, birds chirped, and frogs croaked.

And the light was just shining through a newly weds window.
And I loved all the things that I've done.
And I hoped and I cherished the things I will become.
You can not change any mind unheard.
But, hear us all, here, and fly, and be free.
Like the blue-jays and black-birds, next time.
For the sun rays, and new eyes.
Just Last Monday—
Just last Monday, I sang this, for women like myself.
Just last Monday, I preached, I walked, and I screamed.
Just last Monday, I saw a hundred opportunities.
Just last Monday, I found myself in the world.
Just last Monday, I heard 50 cent on the radio.
Just last Monday, I barked at a dog...
Just last Monday, I was crying from loss.
Just last Monday, I looked for the next.

Just last Monday, I smiled, and thought
to myself.
Just last Monday I had peanuts and ice
cream, and rose hips.
And even on Mondays, I hear you can
help.
Hey, Kid.
Modeling, not for fame.
Not for money or namesakes.
No single expectancy.
Expect changes.
Earthly, or timely?
Lightly.
I could leave everything behind.
For the leopard's skin.
Gnawing and heart-seeking.
For magma, or mothers.
Or American bellied thorn hills.
Great graves, making paint.
Tranquil and falls, then these years
You do your thing, I'll do mine.
*Climbing new kinds of ladders, while you still
have time, kid.*
*Tell them all how you just want to tell them
to shine, kid.*

"Can I Help You?" Saves Lives.
It's my time, now, I'm awake.
I'm just beginning.
Ever growing, every second.
Every beat. I should be thrilled.
Are you with me?
Forever and always.
Breath with all your body.
I don't want to die.
I don't even want to imagine it.
Then imagine the beauty.
All your friends, at this moment.
How they laugh, and show off.
They drive lowriders and pickups.
Or midsize sedans.
They walk familiar streets and go to
church, and meet people like you.
They guffaw when the light shines just
right on their face, in reflections.
They look down, and think, *wow, I got
taller!*
Some are fighting, and winning, with
blood, sweat, and smiles on their faces.
Some are losing, and know that some
days are just days.

Sometimes, you can not remember. And this is perfectly okay...
Things change faster than you think.
And "Can I help you?" saves lives.
For My Sake, And Your Own.
May you be confident with your choice, and read on.
Yet, have caution.
Many others, as I write, have contributed to my understanding of the world.
The city I'm in.
The people I meet.
My lapses in memory.
My family.
My friends.
The lost, and the seeking, who found me.
Pieces of myself, in the world.
Glimpses of knowledge.
For my sake, and your own.
May You—
May you be substantial with your friends.
May your influence and voice break ground.

May your hands move mountains and raise cities.
May your teeth be strong and sharp as steel.
May you progress with every level, every step, every year.
May you find love, and love find you.
May you look down, and see wonderful worlds.
May you seed and sew, each year, and not kill too many plants.
May you learn and eat right.
May you teach, and be taught.
May you find yourself, within all this commotion.
May you know that sometimes, your words feel repetitive.
May you hear their importance each time, to each audience.
May you dance and jump around, shake the house, and sleep well.
May you love the winter frosts from the comfort of your cottons.
May you drink up and celebrate, every year.
May you live.

May you thrive.
My Self.
By myself, I do not feel alone.
My self is by a river.
My self is with friends.
My self is promoting ideals and cultures.
My self is enjoying a beautifully seared
wagyu steak.
My self is in the eyes of many, and in the
air and soil.
My self is in the mind, in the cosmos and
soil.
My self is with you, now, doing
something you love.
My self is with many.
I encourage the same. .
Comfortable.
It's on-lookers.
It's about ferries and fairy tales, or
suitcases and profit margins.
It's the hopeless romantics and flex-
income fathers.
It's engines that purr.
Sometimes, I wander.

Sometimes I wonder where I might be different.
Sometimes the people walking by might shine once,
Sniff twice,
Or they'll stare, if you're lucky,
From open windows, to empty mugs.
To the smell of a fresh Italian roast on the corner.
In Your Wake.
It's been tiring,
so rest well,
Feel well, because your cheeks might feel fuzzy
And so will mine, in your wake.
The Righteous.
You felt different.
You felt righteous.
How I wish I had told you...
How informal, I showed you.
One Day.
Long delays at train stops, and a team.
Their black coat-tailed flew in the trailer hitched mountains.

Like Little John and Robin, telling stories
to get through the lull, our friendships
were moments, still fleeting, wherever I
go.
This was a man saying "rest", and coder,
and a driver, and a keeper.
This was for all of the people that told
me how useless I was when I was alone.
They protect and they guide, they inflict
and misguide.
We see terror you hope not to know of.
So my sister is safe, and my morals are
made to be like all the men that despise.
Still, I must thank them, their strength
and wrongdoings.
Not all can have all.
Not all can see all.
Not all say they're flawed, yet, perfect, a
stretch.
I hope to make use, in a new kind of way.
My pen as a sword, and their swords
could be shields.
And the planet will burst and reign
down...
Someday... My friend.

Me Too.
I would remember it like you.
I would hate how I wanted to be not.
Then, my body would—
Take off.
I'll Keep What's Forever.
I've been low on my luck, and lucky.
I've been grateful, and still, I've been
shamed.
I've said I can take it, then turn, in
abandon.
Hypocrisy bleeds to the surface some
days.
I've had powers that felt superhuman.
I've said things that can not be unsaid.
I've had dreams that I would not
imagine.
I know that my heart is much more than
I let.
We all give, and take, in the end.
We all have hope at some point, in
ourselves.
We all have losses, and gains, so our
gains go to others.
I'll keep what's forever, in bed.

To: Brazen and Tough.
9 is a great age, and age these days, not a number, but a state of mind.
My mind loved to scrape its knees on asphalt, back then.
Not thinking about plasmas or thyroids, but sour gummy worms and $0.99 tea.
I felt limber and lost, I saw passings and coin tosses for pencil erasers and candy.
Here, to brazen, and tough.
Revelations.
Then, time was laid out.
At first, like an equation.
Then, an ever changing road that I walk through the stars, with colors and hues never seen.
An explosion of memories and moments, and a doorway to experience.
Behind, a light, and nothing but a shadow ahead.
Then, a presence, in front of me, that spanned on for miles.
I should see it like valleys, upon my own skin.

Then, falling back into what I feel, here,
on Earth.
Now, my shadow's behind me.
My world, it sits below me.
The surfaces twirl and twist and breath.
At first, I get quite sad—
Then realize, it's not all.
I look around at the less, and I thank, to
my core.
Seasonal Blessings.
I remember how the cherry blossoms
blanket the ground every season, and the
whirlwinds that swept them up in the
air.
I look up to a kitchen that's full of
commotion and chatter.
Then the star on the tree, and full bellies.
Then, the angels.
Men, in their suits, and warm joggers.
Women, with nice bags and glasses.
Red solo cup ragers and hard rock.
Through the walls of the circus, just
dancing.
We danced, too. I remember.

We were silent, like magic, or the blessings that covered our eyes.

.

To: The Spoken.
I now believe I am my shadow. Just a shadow, in life.
My eyes and my breaths might connect me.
I looked in the mirror and saw every man, woman, pupil, and the theft of my words.
As I took pennies for myself, and my words were for others.
So I would like to tell you—
Count, and count well,
Because a count and accounts and a pocket, too.
To fairness and motion.
To earth.
To the spoken.
My Body Is Changing.
With a phone in my pocket, and paper in hand, I take roads that will hopefully guide me.

It's late in the day, and the carbons I eat and breath are paining me.
Change well, for the moment you hope you can say "for the better".
The sun is still shining, and the railroad goes on, and the clouds on horizons are pink, and I laugh.
My body is changing.
Who You Think Of.
Hold on...
I know who you think of when you straighten your back, and I know why I keep guessing these thoughts all wrong.
What is unseen, and unknown...
Somewhere, I know I'm wrong.
Somewhere, I haven't learned.
But a craftsman doesn't throw broken tables or toys, no.
A craftsman might sit alone for hours, tinkering, and tweaking.
A craftsman might be in your mother, or teacher.
I think "God, He knows! And I miss you."
My Mom.

And my pulse said "I'm right here in
front of you."
My Dad.
20 People.
These people are
Like something I've been
Trying to go out
I see
Your message
I've been
Part of
Something I can't see
So somewhere
You are something
Feel how I might have been
Grandfathered into this
News on
Upstairs
Over here, it's family
To music, wow
Chant chakras
Hillsides, sheep and
Rivers flowing
Animal.
On The Shores Above.

Looking down the barrel, a gun.
Then, a walk with the stars, and rum.
A walk to remember a love.
I dock on the shores above.
Manifest In Greatness.
All I need is a little greatness.
Something magnificent.
Something undoubtable.
Meditate.
Meditate it off.
Reach out to the brink of the feeling of
reach.
Feel your weight pull your spine.
Trust in all of the feelings.
Even the fright. Even the anger.
All of the lights that fly by, with
discretion.
For a moment you might love.
A Cure.
Less, for more to come.
A cure, like a nightshade... or getting lost
in myself.
A Drumline.
A drumline.
It's 2025, as the air gets more dense.

A drumline.
I laugh until my rib cage hurts, hand
slamming down on my desk.
Then a drumline.
Cheering courtside, two $8 beers, now,
half split to the ground we didn't notice
was sticking.
Oh, the roar that was heard.
Aahhh ah!
Touchdown.
click
A drumline.
Then polaroids, flapping in the wind.
I'll remember forever.
This drumline.
Bum-dum-tss, da-da-da-dum-tss
Or, during summer, when the meat just
touched down on the foreman.
Ba-dum-tss, da-dum-dum-tss.
At the market, where tills had small corners
of rust building up.
But, our neighbors!
We love them.
A drumline on a night, flying south on i-5.
To the lake?

No, the river!
I don't care! As long as we're free!
A Heart.
Now, my friend.
I will assure you, a heart, it can burst.
You can see them, and read them.
You can trust them, and cherish them.
You can test them, and find them.
You can hold them, and hide them.
You can keep and forgive them.
You can feel, and mistake them.
You drive them, and show them to all
that you know.
We Are Silver Linings.
We are tragedy, and we are symphonies.
We are pain, and we are sympathy.
All that matters is what is lying in the
dark when you are struggling to find the
light.
Maybe, I'll find it with you.
In your green jade necklace or tan
corduroy t-shirt that you've kept since
your father passed away.

In those text messages you re-read, or
the picture framed up on your
nightstand.
In the way you're always okay, for the
world, allowing eyes to penetrate deeper
past the things that have been chained to
your mind, and unto the world you
create, for the sake of the smiles of those
who will ask you, politely.
In your silver linings, in the tune of your
own song.

The Forest.

The forest is quiet.
Snowfall sneaks through the thin
canopy.
The woodpeckers hide under robins and
bears are entranced in their slumber.
Moss covered rocks and the sides of the
trees that get light.
The creek seems still as the deer
approach it, their hooves churning sand
on the shorelines.
"This life." They say to each other. "So
important."

And the fauns look onward, to mother, and bellow.
Their coats all dusted, and shimmering.
"And the small ones. We love them, but still, we need food, so roam on, we must."
And the sun starts to rise. So the robins start singing to all that might hear, like the wolves on their journey to lands far off.
And the wind is still howling at them.
The forest went on for eternities, it seemed.
And the ferns were frost-bitten, and rose hips now dry.
So the squirrels and rabbits sought others, for warmth and for company, as the days disappeared, and nights became long.
And the snake slithered on, smiling, so happy to be among us, in the forest.
The Jungle.
The jungle is loud.
Teeming with water and life.

The tiger roars coming home from his hunt, and his neighbors respect him.
"I see you all." He says. "I bring balance."
And the crickets all echo as the monarch butterfly's return home.
"We are many, and we hope to help you all find what you need, today." They purred in the caves that were dripping sweet moisture.
The air hot, dense, and conforming, it carried the songs of the lemurs in trees that held fruits of all colors.
They were craftsmen, with tools we had known at one time, their long tails and hands all busy at work, or at play.
The jungle never ends, like a dream that you love, or sunset that is burned in the back of your memory.
The chaos ensued, so energetically, and with purpose, as the ferns all untangled for the stick bugs and mantis.
Snakes hissed on their branches above frogs that would cheer them on, knowing well of their safety in the jungle.

Visions.
Like a totem or tombstone.
Or a keystone, or bonfire.
Like a fragrance, or memory.
Like a pillar or bridge that can stabilize,
or connect us.
Like a spirit, or a baseline I hope to be
with, or achieve.
Stupid, and Ingenious.
You try again.
You explain even further.
You strive for it. You believe in it.
*Going for the things you'll never reach, yet
being content.*
Lovin' so hard you might break.
Continuing on, despite all that you hear.
This is stupid, and ingenious, all at once.
These Moments, You'll Cherish.
You're a journey, or explorer, and you're
traveling far to find things that your eyes
have not seen.
Or... I am.
I was?
You may be.

You are a joy in a dream of an ocean of shadows, my friend.
And you are hidden, for now, and in moments you'll cherish.

Repetition.

You are history, and repetition, representing the things we have known to take us further, and backwards, alike.
You're tiny but as grand as life itself, a bit different, each time.
You are growing, and growing, and you can be with us for a moment.
And another.
And another.
And another.

Infinicy.

You are infinicy, and life, full of infancy and strife, but you carry on, whether knee deep in mud or floating on water that is thicker than wine.
There is a staircase we are taking, and the journey is long, and you are complete.
You are what's next and what's new.
You are above and below, somehow.

To Those Beside Me.
The epitome of meaning, defining
yourself how you see as the fittest.
Or bravest.
Or most becoming, explaining yourself to
the ones who might share this.
Who have read this or been this, or
believed this to be all they want or can
know.
This is starlight, and language, and the
beginning, or a memory.
This is born-to-be-something.
Finally, we find this, and hold this so
close to our hearts, like our teachers or
prayers, or hymnals and songs that we
keep in our books, just for safety.
I hope that you know you are hope.
Your strength and your courage, in the
faces of horrors that face us.
You're a long walk beside me at night.
A Lifetime.
What does forever look like?
I think, for a moment, that I can see it,
but then everything shakes and moves

past me, from a focal point far off, then behind.
An explosion of light, full of life, that started nowhere, with no end.
Creation beyond and above, this is what takes us where we love, and where we are destined to be.
An illusion that we chart and try to control, yet with laws and boundaries.
Can I have more, please? I beg of you.
Each Day, A New Day.
Patience, like a child who has yet to grow up and see all for reality, and to find meaning among precious seconds, like opportunities we must seize at first glance.
I lie in bed, for days, as mine seems to have distraught me. I can no longer see any more.
I lie waiting for something, or someone to share some. My eyes on a screen that brings thoughts to me, or a paper that brings stress, but utility, for today.
Today I woke up and I saw more than I did before.
Lessons.

We planned, and pushed through, and we found ourselves backward in memory, as I have yet to see your walls and your hallways, and like plates of silver and gold our thoughts and our people withstand.

We found ourselves screaming at the crowd, or hugging them, as we know that our time here is limited.

We found freedom and resolve, and we broke this in stone so these thoughts would live on.

We founded life here, with expectations that did not account for the time that we would take, or that takes us.

So I've waited. Now what?

I'm in fear of this greatness, I am merely a glimpse, and to share it with you...

But we do share it.

But, for days— —-

Thrive in its boundaries, and gravity. Let them pull in your time.

And do not forget what is important.

Duality of a Creature.

We give perspective to this life.

This perspective can be beautiful.
It might take some time to find it within....
I can see...
I can explain...
Will you do the same?
For our futures to know?
A new kind of society, resembling old.
A new kind of faith.
A dualistic new face.
To the earth that we hold and let fall between fingers, to the light behind the brink of my eyes.
A new planet.
New worlds.
Love, I.
Freshly mown grass, on a Sunday.
Or the bark of my Latin-American friend, not two feet from the ground, as he wags his tail.
Or the purrs from a Bombay, as a kitten, as we lay down for the night in a new home.
Or that finished wooden trim. Or the sound of 8 cylinders.

I went back to the beach, with my
mother, playing hookie, and that time
when I drank so much I passed out, but
somebody was there to save me.
I remember love more than anything,
like running down to the store on the
corner with my sister for gumballs and
soda.
Or the times we would paint, with glitter
and pipe cleaners, making abstract with
folds, and then cutting snowflakes or
smiley faces out.
Or my first kiss in a park, and we fell on
top of each other, after running so hard
our legs gave out.
Then there were my friends, playing
sword-fight with sticks by the creek by
our house, reenacting our favorite heroes
from movies we'd seen, and recreated.
When I see love, I see family visits, on
holidays, to see Oregon's finest
attractions, along with long nights on
the town, or at our old high-school
bleachers, or in the passenger seat of
your car, overlooking the countryside

that was blooming with red clovers and
rhododendrons.
Or I see those games we would play at
our desks, thumbs up, or standing in
corners.
Music used to blare as we drove through
the night, all eyes on the street sides
peeling toward ours.
Then, there was that feeling we all get
after compliments.
We looked good?
We looked great.

Love, II.

We looked sharp on prom night, pinning
corsages on lapels. Familiar tunes drive
us on and we stomp our feet harder,
until sweating. And the roar from the
crowd was unforgettable.
Sharing any, and everything.
And sneaking out just to meet, and to
roam.
Laughing so hard we excuse ourselves
from the classroom, then meet up for the
show, and walk home, still laughing.
With love-letters on desks that made us
so excited we wrote some ourselves.

When I see love, I see the place where
the wolves and the eagles would call to
us, and the hippopotamus would open its
jaws wide, not yawning, but waiting for a
snack.
And the eagles, they were glorious. Over
lakes, they would soar, as we packed
Doritos in our ham and cheese
sandwiches.
We told stories late at night of ghosts
and vampires, or men who fell trees, or
fairy's and druids, or old-world gods
with these powers that seemed other-
worldly, yet familiar.
The next day, we would wake up to the
smell of bacon, and coffee, and come out
to a feast, cooked with love and good
rest.
Celebrating life, and roles, and things
that meant something to Christ, but
now, to us, meant walks among fir trees,
and colorful lights we hung up next to
stars in our kitchen window.
How they glowed on for months.

And how we sang songs together at the
top of our lungs.
Or made calls in the middle of the night,
to escape.
How we got lost in commotion and
chatter, still dazed yet so lively, as these
spirits had always brought us up.
Pushing hair out of our eyes, and looking
up to see smiles.
With bowlfuls of chocolates, or
doughnuts in the break room, just
because we thought "Maybe they'll want
some, too."
We would sit down and work on our
projects together, bouncing ideas back
and forth, because your opinion meant
so much to our product.
Dancing away all the stressors, for our
health, that was out of love.
Passion.
Going out just for pictures, and our
friends in group calls, getting
competitive online.
So many victories and losses that taught
us our know-how.

And our teachers long lectures, and
tangents, from their hearts, and to ours.
And those who would speak up just
because, who could not shut their
mouths, or mouthed off, but in honesty
and compassion.
Lighting fireworks and barbecues, filling
the street with aromas I will never
forget.
All for sights that we shared, and that
live on, through our memory.
Then speaking for those who could not
do the same, but that appreciated
nothing more than the attention and
respects, and silly comments that got us
through our work shifts.
And that look that was shot from across
the room, full of knowing and
expectation, and a drive that set me off
to do things out of love.
How we reconcile and we run to you for
advice when we're hurt, or when lost, or
when we need to hear ourselves.

When our family is gone, and you'd hold us, and whisper sweet things we remember.
We would bask in the sunlight, or hide under covers on cold mornings, when the seasons would change, and leaves fall, or buds bloom, or the snow seemed so bright we'd wake up.
What we ponder alone, and can bring, that is love.
Not granted, but given.
Old Friends.
We are all grown up now.
We used to be rambunctious.
We used to speak out of pocket.
We used to care what others thought.
Of our looks.
Of our status.
With our goals and ambitions set higher than the ceilings of churches or courtrooms, we would fight together, and cry together.
Flying through town, with the sunroofs down, begging to just peek over and into

the gusting wind and rays of summer
heat.
We used to light fires for fun, and burn
sugars from our local 7-11, just for an
excuse to be together, and to spark that
adrenal gland we had just been
discovering.
We used to be faded, and chose to run
from our problems, seeking like-minded
and like-spoken individuals on our short
walks home as a new-blood family.
With essays of soldiers and worms,
religions and mitochondria, foreign
affairs and mental health, we were
sponges that could regurgitate
spontaneity at a whim.
We used to think we knew everything,
and anything between.
Marching on, single file, with
anticipation and excitement in each step.
We used to jump creeks and run laps
around our gymnasium, seeking our
parents in dense crowds, in awe at the
white and red stage lights that illuminate
our moments of success.

We used to hold a spirit that you only
find in the trust of youth.
Now, I am here for you.
Always thinking twice before diving into
anything alone.
Now, we hit strip malls and late-night
shows instead of playgrounds and parks.
Now, we run to purge carbons from our
body, and breathe deeply with each other
at heart.
Now, we drink, and share stories of our
youth that you would only believe if you
were with us yourself.
Now, we are dedicated.
Now, we are entranced in the lull of our
daily routine, always seeking something
for that surge of dopamine behind our
eyes.
Now, we are fine dining, on coffee and
Tylenol, and exchange our raging house
parties for nice talks on our lunch
breaks.
Now, we buy kale and carrots, and care
for the aged hearts that we so longingly
care for.

Now we have children ourselves.
Now, we guess at what you might think
of us, so think twice, as we still feel we
have something to prove.
Now, I think alone has a new meaning.
Family.
Three-thousand-mile flights and twelve
hour road trips for days or weeks of
company celebration.
Dedication to each other, through phone
lines and paper mail.
We love you.
We are always here when you need us.
Here in the heart, I can find you.
We go back to the days on ice skates or
roller blades, or to midnight releases at
the local theater. To the days we would
sit together, in humid heat, planning
grand feasts or long walks within our
communities. To the moments we made
up for screaming at each other so loud
the neighbors grew concerned, or to the
moments we would laugh when we
would fall and scrape our knees.

To me, family is more than blood, though.

Family is the man I see on the roadside that has hit his all-time-low, whose eyes are torn, yet heart remains strong in spite of his losses. The man who will tell you he is alright, and that could ask nothing more than a moment to share.

Family is the woman who walks up to me and gives me her sweater as we are both hiding from sleet and rain in a closed store alcove.

Family is the small, furry creatures who beg for our attention, who we take one glance at in the rescue shelter and think that's the one.

Family loves you. Family sees you and understands you.

We all go back so far, to the chaotic oceans that bred life on this seed of a planet we all share. Family is in the connection we have to the soil we tend to, and to the winds that seem to call our names on quiet hikes through the mountains.

We are all circles of life, and pupils connected through the vast spaces between us, like neurons in our brains, or stars in our galaxy.

From our Fathers and Mothers who placed us here, to our sisters and brothers who walk beside us, to the Children we all must learn to raise. As a family, we all work toward the goal of building our heaven onward, or upward, and bringing all the values we learn from our time here, as humans.

To me, this is family. This is everyone, and this is everything.

Am I To Be Loved?

I sip on a glass, as he sips on a flask.

I walk the pavement as he walks the limestone.

I stumble forward, as does he, and at once, we both speak.

This is too much.

This is not meant for me.

From lawyers to landlords, and from carpenters to convicts, we hear the same thing.

Do I need this?
I hear a cry, then a lecture, then a lady I
know grows more anxious.
She takes my hand, shaking, and says
share this. Give me your pains, give me
your death, as it is better I than you.
But if we drink together, maybe it will be
neither, or both. I think this is good, as
going on should be with you, as should
going out.
These grapevines were meant for many,
and our plates grew so large, from the
palms of our hands to the refrigerators
we fill.
Does the poison say "I am to be loved?"
I fear it, and the day it may overtake me,
as it has for another I know.

A Solution To Smoke.
Particles and changes.
Fire once gave us life.
Fire once gave us heat.
Fire once turned the natural into the
desolate, yet bred life from its ashes.
We once cultivated the branches we
burned and the heaths we would gather

upon, as the smell wafted on for miles,
alerting the world of our company, and
our unique discovery.
Now, I see billions of exhaust pipes.
I see horizons that are dense, full of
colors like the core of our earth.
I see the Amazon causing winds to carry
millions of pounds of toxins and gasses
overhead, and corporations banking off
the tar in our lungs.
I see the oxygen we once cultivated turn
to floods that move cities, and the
branches we once swang from fall to dirt
that we have abandoned.
Oh, how we could go backward in time.
How our greatest achievement must
breed our greatest salvation.
How we must re-till these soils, and find
billions of seeds. How we must share
what we excrete into the world, and how
we must all see the goals together.
When our oceans rise, and our
mountains chip away, how we must find
congregation, and mitigate damage in
communities that should diversify to the
extent they once were.

Oh, world, what can one do?
One is strong, and one's hands can move
matter, and one's breath can take toxins
from the air, purifying and purging, at
the cost of one's time.
My time for another. That is balance.
My lungs may cry out in joy, one day,
knowing what we had done for each
other, and our future, in the cloudy haze
we call present.
Abandonment.
A war of color.
Then, of namesakes.
Then, fate.
All, for bills.
Our parents chimed in, or opposed.
Some have fought, some have chosen to
step aside for the violence.
But, violence, who credits abandonment?
Did we see them?
Did we hear them?
Bystanders, so blinded and numb to the
chaos.
I'll try to find a middle ground, and dig
deep.

A painful reality, to be caught in between those who live faultless and faulty.
Or who say, and feel, such.
The Land I Stand Upon.
I am here for you.
In the moments you need me.
In the moments you don't.
I will defend you.
See your ideals.
See all of your principles.
See you, see others.
See all of the praise and the worship. .
And the land that I stand upon agrees.
A Better Picture.
I feel good, I've won.
I am happy, and of the pure?
Let them forgive me.
Please, do not hate me.
I have struggled, but live on my own, not alone.
We've been hurt, and distracted, and lost, but we'll find our own way.
I would hope alongside you.
To set an example.

To reach out to those that feel beneath you.
To be the guiding hand, or light in the dark.
The mistake of the safest– ignorance, neglect.
You have to dip your toes in all the paint to get a better picture.
Open Eyes.
For furry, feathered friends.
And campfires to come.
For bars and stop–sign corners.
The best is what we chose.
I learned from many fathers.
My mother is a melody and family is not far.
Not everything is flawless,
Less is for the guys that witness all the turmoil.
We smile through open eyes.
Until You're Gray And Old.
I said this to myself.
I was those around.
I was in a game.
I was looking all around.

I don't like to lie, but still, sometimes I get confused.
Your dreams are full of life.
You'll hear, until you're gray and old.
You Don't See What I Do.
All of it matters to you.
There's one when you're ill, and ten in one month.
This can be fun, this can be cool.
Sometimes, when I joke, you don't see how I do.
Sayings.
Confessions.
Pretending.
Sitting.
Humming.
Lessons.
Not lending.
Thinking.
Bumming.
Quiet.
Laying.
Moving.
Staying.
Paying.

Relaying
Impressions.
Sayings.
What We Build.
Maybe I'm not perfect.
Maybe I'm a vivid dream.
Maybe I put all this down to paper to
believe.
*Maybe I can hear you somewhere you might
never go.*
We take another walk, look down, and
smile, for the road.
Steering on this beautifully built cosmic
light equation.
I'll let go of what I've seen, if what we
build is more important.
Far Away.
It's only one day.
It's only one story.
It's only one step on a line.
Another one may, and another got gory.
Still, I've been stuck on those eyes.
Far away.
I don't want to run from all the pain.
But I don't want to be stationed here.

I don't want to be lost here.
Far away.
I don't want to walk inside the pain.
I don't want to go without you.
By my side, no doubt.
What Am I?
I move, I breed.
I rise. I fall.
I freeze and shiver..
I wash and meander.
I give and I take.
I run, yet I'm still.
I change, yet remain.
I grow, and disappear.
You're blood.
You're bone.
Your breaths, and on stone.
You're cloud and you're shade, through
night and through day.
You're ours, and you're yours.
You're needed, you're terror.
You're blue, yet so bright, O' being of
Life.
You're true and you're light.
You're calm and so righteous.

You live on with moments we hope to
keep alive.
I Struggled To Make Any Sounds.
The treasure I guard
with fists balled up
and heels dug deep in the ground
are like friends I loved
and forgot with the days that I struggled
to make any sound.
Clearly, and Slow.
Your eyes can speak.
Your eyes can shine.
Your eyes can stretch from head to toe.
Still, I instill a commitment.
I might have told one, but ten overheard.
Kneading foreign grain breads, I rumble
my dream, above and below.
I could anoint you a friend, I say to
myself, clearly, and slow.
Come A Little Closer.
Lilac on the summer breeze.
Dew drops on the ferns.
Back when life felt easy.
Beaches, I sat, to discern.
I'll consider it a little closer.

I'll try my best to remember.
Inside me, burning, fire, and flickering quick.
There's lots to learn.
We tried to get you higher
We tried, and tired, and tried.
Please come a little closer.
To: You.
I promise, to You.
I'm here, for You
I'll be stronger than I was before.
I'll be patient and write to You.
I'm here for You.
I'll follow, I'll stay right behind, for you.
I'll sacrifice all of this time, for you.
Your Mother And your Father.
Try, for the people to come.
Try to be people you come from.
Tell me what you've become.
They say you're just like your mother and your father.
Like a lion, we're seeking horizons.
We try to not forget them when we run from our lives.

Do you dare to be a part of all the secrets
that we are,
not the perfect little people we never say
we aren't?
Tell your story to the night.
Tell a friend about a time.
They say you're not at all your mother or
your father.
The Trees I See.
Time throughout my life lights up like
trees.

Look, here, I'm dust!
We teach this, too!
Here, awake, then shake,
Seconds — -
What can I see?
I'm rooted in family, and hills, and ferns, and
soil and seed.
Oh, Animal Person, Oh, Human I see.
Your eyes might pour like faucet drains and—
-
Time, I'm glad I face it.
Time not wasted, spend it here with me.
The World.

From the Heavens we chisel in stone, to
the ships we're calling our home.
The sun could be from my Father, and
my Mother could be where I roam.
I Am Connected.
I am deep.
I am galactic.
I am the cosmos.
I am the planet.
I am unlike the things I've seen.
Close isn't the same, to me.
I'm rough on the edges, to you.
To me, the same.
To us, it's just names.
I am predictive.
I am inventive
I am melodic.
I am sequential.
You'll run with the veterans.
You'll hum all the lessons.
Recite all the miles.
Recite, for your brethren.
Speak with the sun, and speak to
yourself.
Love how it all comes down to this.

I am the sun.
I am the shadow.
More than just one.
I am connected.
I Am Them.
I am you.
I am him.
I am her.
I am dead.
I am truth and language.
I am the melody, here in the head.
I am youth.
I am sin.
I am truth.
I'm with them.
I love all this broken language.
Broken body, broken bed.
I am You.
I am Him.
I am You .
I am Them.
You Still Have Your Soul.
See my eyes.
I know you told your friends.
I meant to hide.

My fever dreams kept me up at night.
You check.
Your head is spinning.
Such a perfect thing.
One can get too high.
Just take it easy soldier, we don't cry alone.
You still have your heart, soldier, you
still have your soul.
Drones.
Drones.
I'm humming.
Humming, humming.
Homes.
I'm coming.
Coming, coming.
Visions.
Becoming, changing, and loving.
Minds.
They're humming.
Humming, humming.
The Red Ones.
Cool, by envisions it is healing an incision
with its fingernails and bitterness.
Pour me up a red one.

*Aiming with precision and seeing my
decision and seeing the world like the little
ones and bitter ones.*
I love the red ones.
I Feel Alive.
Scream.
Go ahead, beam it.
Dream.
Just believe in them.
Breath.
We're so alive.
See.
I feel alive.
All Of The Beauty You Have To Unfold.
You've been strong for miles...
You've got a way to go...
Resilience comes from pain.
Like water, it comes and goes.
Don't be scared to ask us.
Don't be scared to shout.
*Don't be scared to look onward at all of the
beauty you have to unfold.*
A Stressful September.
I made a bet, *maybe I will save him.*
I took a loan, *baby I hated it.*

I took a drug, *baby I made it.*
Baby, I made it, *baby, we made it.*
I got a job, *maybe I like him.*
I hit the road, *he's a shit typer.*
I hit a low, *I met a stranger*
I hit a wall, *I think I'm in danger.*
I think I'm in love, *I think I'll let him.*
I need a shove, *he's cool like my temper.*
Seven or eight? *I can't remember.*
I can't remember a *stressful September.*
Forever We'll Dream—
Forever I'll listen for birds.
Forever I'll talk to the skies.
Forever, I'll see dragonflies, oceans, and
all of the things that I like.
I learned that I'm building Heaven.
I built it with you and your eyes.
I built it with you, and your Heaven.
Forever we'll dream, ever old.
Feline Type.
Shiny white.
All my might,
Eve of night.
Tools for life.
If just to fight?

If just to bite.
Place them nicely.
Use them right.
Be: Now.
Go *out.*
Speak, *shout.*
Big dog, *peace?*
See ? *Wow.*
Swoop. Bow.
Teeth proud.
Bone, ow.
Endow.
No frown keep thou.
Me? *Now.*
Be : *Now.*
Hands.
Closed.
Open.
In your face.
On your shoulder, then your waist.
To show, to tell.
To keep, or forsake .
To love, and to hold.
To wave, and to shake.
The Way You Think.

With all of the time that I have and all
the things that I think.
With all who I might meet, no money
could make me break.
I could show you the world I see.
It's beautiful, I think.
In comfort, I could sink.
I could show you the things I need.
Oh, the things I need are so simple like
you and me.
All your sympathy, let it wash over me.
I love the way you think.
I love the way you drink.
Only You.
Hello, and goodbye, to you.
Through all of my time, to you.
There is strength inside you.
Only you can find you.
Adored.
In walks a king and a joke.
The king had knotted his hope.
You are akin to the folk.
So, I am a human, I know.
Are you laughing?
Are you with me?

Bring us a storm.
The bounty was not for corn.
We've found a place to mourn.
You're desperate and bored.
You're not?
I am.
I have been secretly sworn at.
I have been secretly torn.
I shimmer, and pour.
I'm rare, and I'm bored.
I'm stuck in a habit.
I'm with you.
Adored.
To: All Those In Recovery.
I pledge allegiance to the flag...
And all those in recovery.
And to the republic, for which it stands...
For the land and peace for all.
Indivisible...
Until I fall.
A Typical Ride.
I love to look up to the sun.
I love to look up to the sky.
I love to look up to the songs.
I never, no never, will lie to you.

Maybe, I fall in the night.
Maybe, I fake a disguise.
I want to be nice.
A typical ride.
So Blue.
I knew.
I flew.
Vocations, "I do."
There's things that I wanted, and things
that I used.
My heart, my hue, and my bag, to boots.
That is so you, and so perfect, so blue.
I knew.
I flew on vacation with you.
Sometimes my bite leaves me too much
to chew.
My fire, my hue, and my bag, to my
boots.
That is so you.
Like the sky, so blue.
Don't Silence My Heart.
Don't silence my heart.
I won't.
Like lions, we keep and face the dark.

Leaders don't level our cities, make
hydrogen into a war crime like an art.
These gasses in masses, and masks, and
we're scared to go out
Cause they're preying on us like sharks!
Somebody save us!
We're trying!
Unable to wake them all up, I'll probably
dart.
I could restart.
I could embark.
I could be scared, or I could remark.
I'd Kind Of Like To—
Tell me what you said when your forever was
through.
You think I'm a terror, I think I could
love you.
See me fly away, I'll fly away when I'm
through.
I'd kind of like to.
Tell me what was said when your life was
through.
You think I'm a servant?
I'm a servant to you.

If this story ever, ever, ever gets
through...
I'll make it to you...
I'll make this to: you...

guitar and maraca interlude

www.ingramcontent.com/pod-product-compliance
Lightning Source LLC
Chambersburg PA
CBHW071516220526
45472CB00003B/1044